ARCHERY SCORE SHEETS

ARCHERY SCORE CARD

Name:

Date:

Distance (m):

Target Face (cm):

Team:

Round:

Ends	Arrows						Scores
	1	2	3	4	5	6	
1							
2							
3							
4							
5							
6							
7							
8							
9							
10							
11							
12							
13							
14							

ARCHERY SCORE CARD

Name:
Date:
Distance (m):
Team:
Target Face (cm):
Round:

Ends	Arrows						Scores
	1	2	3	4	5	6	
1							
2							
3							
4							
5							
6							
7							
8							
9							
10							
11							
12							
13							
14							

ARCHERY SCORE CARD

Name:
Date:
Distance (m): Team:
Target Face (cm): Round:

Ends	Arrows						Scores
	1	2	3	4	5	6	
1							
2							
3							
4							
5							
6							
7							
8							
9							
10							
11							
12							
13							
14							

ARCHERY SCORE CARD

Name:
Date:
Distance (m):
Target Face (cm):
Team:
Round:

Ends	Arrows						Scores
	1	2	3	4	5	6	
1							
2							
3							
4							
5							
6							
7							
8							
9							
10							
11							
12							
13							
14							

ARCHERY SCORE CARD

Name:

Date:

Distance (m):   Team:

Target Face (cm):   Round:

Ends	Arrows						Scores
	1	2	3	4	5	6	
1							
2							
3							
4							
5							
6							
7							
8							
9							
10							
11							
12							
13							
14							

ARCHERY SCORE CARD

Name: _____

Date: _____

Distance (m): _____ Team: _____

Target Face (cm): _____ Round: _____

Ends	Arrows						Scores
	1	2	3	4	5	6	
1							
2							
3							
4							
5							
6							
7							
8							
9							
10							
11							
12							
13							
14							

ARCHERY SCORE CARD

Name:

Date:

Distance (m):

Target Face (cm):

Team:

Round:

Ends	Arrows						Scores
	1	2	3	4	5	6	
1							
2							
3							
4							
5							
6							
7							
8							
9							
10							
11							
12							
13							
14							

ARCHERY SCORE CARD

Name

Date

Distance (m)

Target Face (cm)

Team

Round

Ends	Arrows						Scores
	1	2	3	4	5	6	
1							
2							
3							
4							
5							
6							
7							
8							
9							
10							
11							
12							
13							
14							

ARCHERY SCORE CARD

Name:

Date:

Distance (m):

Target Face (cm):

Team:

Round:

Ends	Arrows						Scores
	1	2	3	4	5	6	
1							
2							
3							
4							
5							
6							
7							
8							
9							
10							
11							
12							
13							
14							

ARCHERY SCORE CARD

Name:
Date:
Distance (m):
Target Face (cm):
Team:
Round:

Ends	\multicolumn{6}{c	}{Arrows}	Scores
	1	2	3	4	5	6	
1							
2							
3							
4							
5							
6							
7							
8							
9							
10							
11							
12							
13							
14							

ARCHERY SCORE CARD

Name:

Date:

Distance (m):   Team:

Target Face (cm):   Round:

Ends	Arrows						Scores
	1	2	3	4	5	6	
1							
2							
3							
4							
5							
6							
7							
8							
9							
10							
11							
12							
13							
14							

ARCHERY SCORE CARD

Name: _____

Date: _____

Distance (m): _____ Team: _____

Target Face (cm): _____ Round: _____

Ends	Arrows						Scores
	1	2	3	4	5	6	
1							
2							
3							
4							
5							
6							
7							
8							
9							
10							
11							
12							
13							
14							

ARCHERY SCORE CARD

Name:

Date:

Distance (m):

Target Face (cm):

Team:

Round:

Ends	Arrows						Scores
	1	2	3	4	5	6	
1							
2							
3							
4							
5							
6							
7							
8							
9							
10							
11							
12							
13							
14							

ARCHERY SCORE CARD

Name

Date

Distance (m)

Target Face (cm)

Team

Round

Ends	Arrows						Scores
	1	2	3	4	5	6	
1							
2							
3							
4							
5							
6							
7							
8							
9							
10							
11							
12							
13							
14							

ARCHERY SCORE CARD

Name

Date

Distance (m)　　　　　　Team

Target Face (cm)　　　　Round

Ends	Arrows						Scores
	1	2	3	4	5	6	
1							
2							
3							
4							
5							
6							
7							
8							
9							
10							
11							
12							
13							
14							

ARCHERY SCORE CARD

Name

Date

Distance (m)

Team

Target Face (cm)

Round

Ends	Arrows						Scores
	1	2	3	4	5	6	
1							
2							
3							
4							
5							
6							
7							
8							
9							
10							
11							
12							
13							
14							

ARCHERY SCORE CARD

Name:
Date:
Distance (m):
Target Face (cm):
Team:
Round:

Ends	Arrows						Scores
	1	2	3	4	5	6	
1							
2							
3							
4							
5							
6							
7							
8							
9							
10							
11							
12							
13							
14							

ARCHERY SCORE CARD

Name

Date

Distance (m)

Target Face (cm)

Team

Round

Ends	Arrows						Scores
	1	2	3	4	5	6	
1							
2							
3							
4							
5							
6							
7							
8							
9							
10							
11							
12							
13							
14							

ARCHERY SCORE CARD

Name:

Date:

Distance (m):

Target Face (cm):

Team:

Round:

Ends	Arrows						Scores
	1	2	3	4	5	6	
1							
2							
3							
4							
5							
6							
7							
8							
9							
10							
11							
12							
13							
14							

ARCHERY SCORE CARD

Name:

Date:

Distance (m):

Target Face (cm):

Team:

Round:

Ends	Arrows						Scores
	1	2	3	4	5	6	
1							
2							
3							
4							
5							
6							
7							
8							
9							
10							
11							
12							
13							
14							

ARCHERY SCORE CARD

Name:

Date:

Distance (m): | Team:

Target Face (cm): | Round:

Ends	Arrows						Scores
	1	2	3	4	5	6	
1							
2							
3							
4							
5							
6							
7							
8							
9							
10							
11							
12							
13							
14							

ARCHERY SCORE CARD

Name: _____

Date: _____

Distance (m): _____ Team: _____

Target Face (cm): _____ Round: _____

Ends	\multicolumn{6}{c}{Arrows}	Scores
	1	2	3	4	5	6	
1							
2							
3							
4							
5							
6							
7							
8							
9							
10							
11							
12							
13							
14							

ARCHERY SCORE CARD

Name:
Date:
Distance (m):
Target Face (cm):
Team:
Round:

Ends	Arrows						Scores
	1	2	3	4	5	6	
1							
2							
3							
4							
5							
6							
7							
8							
9							
10							
11							
12							
13							
14							

ARCHERY SCORE CARD

Name

Date

Distance (m)

Team

Target Face (cm)

Round

Ends	Arrows						Scores
	1	2	3	4	5	6	
1							
2							
3							
4							
5							
6							
7							
8							
9							
10							
11							
12							
13							
14							

ARCHERY SCORE CARD

Name

Date

Distance (m)　　　　　Team

Target Face (cm)　　　Round

Ends	Arrows						Scores
	1	2	3	4	5	6	
1							
2							
3							
4							
5							
6							
7							
8							
9							
10							
11							
12							
13							
14							

ARCHERY SCORE CARD

Name

Date

Distance (m)

Team

Target Face (cm)

Round

Ends	Arrows						Scores
	1	2	3	4	5	6	
1							
2							
3							
4							
5							
6							
7							
8							
9							
10							
11							
12							
13							
14							

ARCHERY SCORE CARD

Name:
Date:
Distance (m):
Target Face (cm):
Team:
Round:

Ends	Arrows						Scores
	1	2	3	4	5	6	
1							
2							
3							
4							
5							
6							
7							
8							
9							
10							
11							
12							
13							
14							

ARCHERY SCORE CARD

Name

Date

Distance (m)

Target Face (cm)

Team

Round

Ends	Arrows						Scores
	1	2	3	4	5	6	
1							
2							
3							
4							
5							
6							
7							
8							
9							
10							
11							
12							
13							
14							

ARCHERY SCORE CARD

Name

Date

Distance (m) Team

Target Face (cm) Round

Ends	Arrows						Scores
	1	2	3	4	5	6	
1							
2							
3							
4							
5							
6							
7							
8							
9							
10							
11							
12							
13							
14							

ARCHERY SCORE CARD

Name

Date

Distance (m)   Team

Target Face (cm)   Round

Ends	\multicolumn{6}{c	}{Arrows}	Scores

Ends	1	2	3	4	5	6	Scores
1							
2							
3							
4							
5							
6							
7							
8							
9							
10							
11							
12							
13							
14							

ARCHERY SCORE CARD

Name:

Date:

Distance (m):

Target Face (cm):

Team:

Round:

Ends	Arrows						Scores
	1	2	3	4	5	6	
1							
2							
3							
4							
5							
6							
7							
8							
9							
10							
11							
12							
13							
14							

ARCHERY SCORE CARD

Name: _____

Date: _____

Distance (m): _____ Team: _____

Target Face (cm): _____ Round: _____

Ends	Arrows						Scores
	1	2	3	4	5	6	
1							
2							
3							
4							
5							
6							
7							
8							
9							
10							
11							
12							
13							
14							

ARCHERY SCORE CARD

Name: _____

Date: _____

Distance (m): _____ Team: _____

Target Face (cm): _____ Round: _____

Ends	\multicolumn{6}{c	}{Arrows}	Scores
	1	2	3	4	5	6	
1							
2							
3							
4							
5							
6							
7							
8							
9							
10							
11							
12							
13							
14							

ARCHERY SCORE CARD

Name: _____

Date: _____

Distance (m): _____ Team: _____

Target Face (cm): _____ Round: _____

Ends	\multicolumn{6}{c}{Arrows}	Scores
	1	2	3	4	5	6	
1							
2							
3							
4							
5							
6							
7							
8							
9							
10							
11							
12							
13							
14							

ARCHERY SCORE CARD

Name

Date

Distance (m)

Target Face (cm)

Team

Round

Ends	Arrows						Scores
	1	2	3	4	5	6	
1							
2							
3							
4							
5							
6							
7							
8							
9							
10							
11							
12							
13							
14							

ARCHERY SCORE CARD

Name

Date

Distance (m)

Target Face (cm)

Team

Round

Ends	Arrows						Scores
	1	2	3	4	5	6	
1							
2							
3							
4							
5							
6							
7							
8							
9							
10							
11							
12							
13							
14							

ARCHERY SCORE CARD

Name: _____

Date: _____

Distance (m): _____ Team: _____

Target Face (cm): _____ Round: _____

Ends	Arrows						Scores
	1	2	3	4	5	6	
1							
2							
3							
4							
5							
6							
7							
8							
9							
10							
11							
12							
13							
14							

ARCHERY SCORE CARD

Name:

Date:

Distance (m):

Target Face (cm):

Team:

Round:

Ends	Arrows						Scores
	1	2	3	4	5	6	
1							
2							
3							
4							
5							
6							
7							
8							
9							
10							
11							
12							
13							
14							

ARCHERY SCORE CARD

Name:

Date:

Distance (m):   Team:

Target Face (cm):   Round:

Ends	Arrows						Scores
	1	2	3	4	5	6	
1							
2							
3							
4							
5							
6							
7							
8							
9							
10							
11							
12							
13							
14							

ARCHERY SCORE CARD

Name: _____

Date: _____

Distance (m): _____ | Team: _____

Target Face (cm): _____ | Round: _____

Ends	\multicolumn{6}{c	}{Arrows}	Scores
	1	2	3	4	5	6	
1							
2							
3							
4							
5							
6							
7							
8							
9							
10							
11							
12							
13							
14							

ARCHERY SCORE CARD

Name:

Date:

Distance (m):   Team:

Target Face (cm):   Round:

Ends	Arrows						Scores
	1	2	3	4	5	6	
1							
2							
3							
4							
5							
6							
7							
8							
9							
10							
11							
12							
13							
14							

ARCHERY SCORE CARD

Name

Date

Distance (m) Team

Target Face (cm) Round

Ends	\multicolumn{6}{c}{Arrows}	Scores
	1	2	3	4	5	6	
1							
2							
3							
4							
5							
6							
7							
8							
9							
10							
11							
12							
13							
14							

ARCHERY SCORE CARD

Name

Date

Distance (m)

Team

Target Face (cm)

Round

Ends	Arrows						Scores
	1	2	3	4	5	6	
1							
2							
3							
4							
5							
6							
7							
8							
9							
10							
11							
12							
13							
14							

ARCHERY SCORE CARD

Name: _____

Date: _____

Distance (m): _____ Team: _____

Target Face (cm): _____ Round: _____

Ends	Arrows						Scores
	1	2	3	4	5	6	
1							
2							
3							
4							
5							
6							
7							
8							
9							
10							
11							
12							
13							
14							

ARCHERY SCORE CARD

Name:

Date:

Distance (m):

Team:

Target Face (cm):

Round:

Ends	Arrows						Scores
	1	2	3	4	5	6	
1							
2							
3							
4							
5							
6							
7							
8							
9							
10							
11							
12							
13							
14							

ARCHERY SCORE CARD

Name:

Date:

Distance (m):

Target Face (cm):

Team:

Round:

Ends	Arrows						Scores
	1	2	3	4	5	6	
1							
2							
3							
4							
5							
6							
7							
8							
9							
10							
11							
12							
13							
14							

ARCHERY SCORE CARD

Name:

Date:

Distance (m):

Target Face (cm):

Team:

Round:

Ends	Arrows						Scores
	1	2	3	4	5	6	
1							
2							
3							
4							
5							
6							
7							
8							
9							
10							
11							
12							
13							
14							

ARCHERY SCORE CARD

Name:

Date:

Distance (m):

Team:

Target Face (cm):

Round:

Ends	Arrows						Scores
	1	2	3	4	5	6	
1							
2							
3							
4							
5							
6							
7							
8							
9							
10							
11							
12							
13							
14							

ARCHERY SCORE CARD

Name:

Date:

Distance (m):   Team:

Target Face (cm):   Round:

Ends	\multicolumn{6}{c}{Arrows}	Scores
	1	2	3	4	5	6	
1							
2							
3							
4							
5							
6							
7							
8							
9							
10							
11							
12							
13							
14							

ARCHERY SCORE CARD

Name

Date

Distance (m)

Target Face (cm)

Team

Round

Ends	Arrows						Scores
	1	2	3	4	5	6	
1							
2							
3							
4							
5							
6							
7							
8							
9							
10							
11							
12							
13							
14							

ARCHERY SCORE CARD

Name:
Date:
Distance (m):
Target Face (cm):
Team:
Round:

Ends	Arrows						Scores
	1	2	3	4	5	6	
1							
2							
3							
4							
5							
6							
7							
8							
9							
10							
11							
12							
13							
14							

ARCHERY SCORE CARD

Name

Date

Distance (m)

Target Face (cm)

Team

Round

Ends	Arrows						Scores
	1	2	3	4	5	6	
1							
2							
3							
4							
5							
6							
7							
8							
9							
10							
11							
12							
13							
14							

ARCHERY SCORE CARD

Name:

Date:

Distance (m):   Team:

Target Face (cm):   Round:

Ends	\multicolumn{6}{c}{Arrows}	Scores
	1	2	3	4	5	6	
1							
2							
3							
4							
5							
6							
7							
8							
9							
10							
11							
12							
13							
14							

ARCHERY SCORE CARD

Name

Date

Distance (m)   Team

Target Face (cm)   Round

Ends	Arrows						Scores
	1	2	3	4	5	6	
1							
2							
3							
4							
5							
6							
7							
8							
9							
10							
11							
12							
13							
14							

ARCHERY SCORE CARD

Name

Date

Distance (m)　　　　　　Team

Target Face (cm)　　　　Round

Ends	Arrows						Scores
	1	2	3	4	5	6	
1							
2							
3							
4							
5							
6							
7							
8							
9							
10							
11							
12							
13							
14							

ARCHERY SCORE CARD

Name

Date

Distance (m)

Target Face (cm)

Team

Round

Ends	Arrows						Scores
	1	2	3	4	5	6	
1							
2							
3							
4							
5							
6							
7							
8							
9							
10							
11							
12							
13							
14							

ARCHERY SCORE CARD

Name:

Date:

Distance (m): Team:

Target Face (cm): Round:

Ends	Arrows						Scores
	1	2	3	4	5	6	
1							
2							
3							
4							
5							
6							
7							
8							
9							
10							
11							
12							
13							
14							

ARCHERY SCORE CARD

Name:

Date:

Distance (m):

Target Face (cm):

Team:

Round:

Ends	\multicolumn{6}{c}{Arrows}	Scores
	1	2	3	4	5	6	
1							
2							
3							
4							
5							
6							
7							
8							
9							
10							
11							
12							
13							
14							

ARCHERY SCORE CARD

Name: _____

Date: _____

Distance (m): _____ Team: _____

Target Face (cm): _____ Round: _____

Ends	Arrows						Scores
	1	2	3	4	5	6	
1							
2							
3							
4							
5							
6							
7							
8							
9							
10							
11							
12							
13							
14							

ARCHERY SCORE CARD

Name: _____

Date: _____

Distance (m): _____   Team: _____

Target Face (cm): _____   Round: _____

Ends	\multicolumn{6}{c	}{Arrows}	Scores
	1	2	3	4	5	6	
1							
2							
3							
4							
5							
6							
7							
8							
9							
10							
11							
12							
13							
14							

ARCHERY SCORE CARD

Name:

Date:

Distance (m): | Team:

Target Face (cm): | Round:

Ends	Arrows						Scores
	1	2	3	4	5	6	
1							
2							
3							
4							
5							
6							
7							
8							
9							
10							
11							
12							
13							
14							

ARCHERY SCORE CARD

Name:
Date:
Distance (m):
Team:
Target Face (cm):
Round:

Ends	\multicolumn{6}{c}{Arrows}	Scores
	1	2	3	4	5	6	
1							
2							
3							
4							
5							
6							
7							
8							
9							
10							
11							
12							
13							
14							

ARCHERY SCORE CARD

Name:

Date:

Distance (m):

Target Face (cm):

Team:

Round:

Ends	Arrows						Scores
	1	2	3	4	5	6	
1							
2							
3							
4							
5							
6							
7							
8							
9							
10							
11							
12							
13							
14							

ARCHERY SCORE CARD

Name:

Date:

Distance (m):

Target Face (cm):

Team:

Round:

Ends	Arrows						Scores
	1	2	3	4	5	6	
1							
2							
3							
4							
5							
6							
7							
8							
9							
10							
11							
12							
13							
14							

ARCHERY SCORE CARD

Name
Date
Distance (m) Team
Target Face (cm) Round

Ends	\multicolumn{6}{c}{Arrows}	Scores
	1	2	3	4	5	6	
1							
2							
3							
4							
5							
6							
7							
8							
9							
10							
11							
12							
13							
14							

ARCHERY SCORE CARD

Name: _____

Date: _____

Distance (m): _____ Team: _____

Target Face (cm): _____ Round: _____

Ends	Arrows						Scores
	1	2	3	4	5	6	
1							
2							
3							
4							
5							
6							
7							
8							
9							
10							
11							
12							
13							
14							

ARCHERY SCORE CARD

Name: _____

Date: _____

Distance (m): _____ Team: _____

Target Face (cm): _____ Round: _____

Ends	Arrows						Scores
	1	2	3	4	5	6	
1							
2							
3							
4							
5							
6							
7							
8							
9							
10							
11							
12							
13							
14							

ARCHERY SCORE CARD

Name:

Date:

Distance (m):

Target Face (cm):

Team:

Round:

Ends	\multicolumn{6}{c	}{Arrows}	Scores
	1	2	3	4	5	6	
1							
2							
3							
4							
5							
6							
7							
8							
9							
10							
11							
12							
13							
14							

ARCHERY SCORE CARD

Name:
Date:
Distance (m):
Target Face (cm):
Team:
Round:

Ends	Arrows						Scores
	1	2	3	4	5	6	
1							
2							
3							
4							
5							
6							
7							
8							
9							
10							
11							
12							
13							
14							

ARCHERY SCORE CARD

Name:
Date:
Distance (m):
Target Face (cm):
Team:
Round:

Ends	Arrows						Scores
	1	2	3	4	5	6	
1							
2							
3							
4							
5							
6							
7							
8							
9							
10							
11							
12							
13							
14							

ARCHERY SCORE CARD

Name: _____

Date: _____

Distance (m): _____ Team: _____

Target Face (cm): _____ Round: _____

Ends	Arrows						Scores
	1	2	3	4	5	6	
1							
2							
3							
4							
5							
6							
7							
8							
9							
10							
11							
12							
13							
14							

ARCHERY SCORE CARD

Name

Date

Distance (m)

Target Face (cm)

Team

Round

Ends	Arrows						Scores
	1	2	3	4	5	6	
1							
2							
3							
4							
5							
6							
7							
8							
9							
10							
11							
12							
13							
14							

ARCHERY SCORE CARD

Name:

Date:

Distance (m):   Team:

Target Face (cm):   Round:

Ends	Arrows						Scores
	1	2	3	4	5	6	
1							
2							
3							
4							
5							
6							
7							
8							
9							
10							
11							
12							
13							
14							

ARCHERY SCORE CARD

Name: _____

Date: _____

Distance (m): _____ | Team: _____

Target Face (cm): _____ | Round: _____

Ends	Arrows						Scores
	1	2	3	4	5	6	
1							
2							
3							
4							
5							
6							
7							
8							
9							
10							
11							
12							
13							
14							

ARCHERY SCORE CARD

Name:

Date:

Distance (m):

Target Face (cm):

Team:

Round:

Ends	Arrows						Scores
	1	2	3	4	5	6	
1							
2							
3							
4							
5							
6							
7							
8							
9							
10							
11							
12							
13							
14							

ARCHERY SCORE CARD

Name

Date

Distance (m)

Team

Target Face (cm)

Round

Ends	Arrows						Scores
	1	2	3	4	5	6	
1							
2							
3							
4							
5							
6							
7							
8							
9							
10							
11							
12							
13							
14							

ARCHERY SCORE CARD

Name:
Date:
Distance (m):
Team:
Target Face (cm):
Round:

Ends	Arrows						Scores
	1	2	3	4	5	6	
1							
2							
3							
4							
5							
6							
7							
8							
9							
10							
11							
12							
13							
14							

ARCHERY SCORE CARD

Name

Date

Distance (m)

Target Face (cm)

Team

Round

Ends	Arrows						Scores
	1	2	3	4	5	6	
1							
2							
3							
4							
5							
6							
7							
8							
9							
10							
11							
12							
13							
14							

ARCHERY SCORE CARD

Name

Date

Distance (m)   Team

Target Face (cm)   Round

Ends	Arrows						Scores
	1	2	3	4	5	6	
1							
2							
3							
4							
5							
6							
7							
8							
9							
10							
11							
12							
13							
14							

ARCHERY SCORE CARD

Name:

Date:

Distance (m):

Target Face (cm):

Team:

Round:

Ends	Arrows						Scores
	1	2	3	4	5	6	
1							
2							
3							
4							
5							
6							
7							
8							
9							
10							
11							
12							
13							
14							

ARCHERY SCORE CARD

Name:

Date:

Distance (m): Team:

Target Face (cm): Round:

Ends	Arrows						Scores
	1	2	3	4	5	6	
1							
2							
3							
4							
5							
6							
7							
8							
9							
10							
11							
12							
13							
14							

ARCHERY SCORE CARD

Name: _____

Date: _____

Distance (m): _____ Team: _____

Target Face (cm): _____ Round: _____

Ends	Arrows						Scores
	1	2	3	4	5	6	
1							
2							
3							
4							
5							
6							
7							
8							
9							
10							
11							
12							
13							
14							

ARCHERY SCORE CARD

Name:
Date:
Distance (m): 　　　　　Team:
Target Face (cm): 　　　Round:

Ends	\multicolumn{6}{c	}{Arrows}	Scores
	1	2	3	4	5	6	
1							
2							
3							
4							
5							
6							
7							
8							
9							
10							
11							
12							
13							
14							

ARCHERY SCORE CARD

Name

Date

Distance (m)

Team

Target Face (cm)

Round

Ends	Arrows						Scores
	1	2	3	4	5	6	
1							
2							
3							
4							
5							
6							
7							
8							
9							
10							
11							
12							
13							
14							

ARCHERY SCORE CARD

Name:
Date:
Distance (m):   Team:
Target Face (cm):   Round:

Ends	Arrows						Scores
	1	2	3	4	5	6	
1							
2							
3							
4							
5							
6							
7							
8							
9							
10							
11							
12							
13							
14							

ARCHERY SCORE CARD

Name:

Date:

Distance (m):   Team:

Target Face (cm):   Round:

Ends	\multicolumn{6}{c}{Arrows}	Scores

Ends	1	2	3	4	5	6	Scores
1							
2							
3							
4							
5							
6							
7							
8							
9							
10							
11							
12							
13							
14							

ARCHERY SCORE CARD

Name:

Date:

Distance (m): 　　　　Team:

Target Face (cm): 　　Round:

Ends	\multicolumn{6}{c	}{Arrows}	Scores
	1	2	3	4	5	6	
1							
2							
3							
4							
5							
6							
7							
8							
9							
10							
11							
12							
13							
14							

ARCHERY SCORE CARD

Name

Date

Distance (m)

Target Face (cm)

Team

Round

Ends	Arrows						Scores
	1	2	3	4	5	6	
1							
2							
3							
4							
5							
6							
7							
8							
9							
10							
11							
12							
13							
14							

ARCHERY SCORE CARD

Name:
Date:
Distance (m):
Target Face (cm):
Team:
Round:

Ends	\multicolumn{6}{c	}{Arrows}	Scores
	1	2	3	4	5	6	
1							
2							
3							
4							
5							
6							
7							
8							
9							
10							
11							
12							
13							
14							

ARCHERY SCORE CARD

Name

Date

Distance (m)

Target Face (cm)

Team

Round

Ends	Arrows						Scores
	1	2	3	4	5	6	
1							
2							
3							
4							
5							
6							
7							
8							
9							
10							
11							
12							
13							
14							

ARCHERY SCORE CARD

Name:

Date:

Distance (m):   Team:

Target Face (cm):   Round:

Ends	\multicolumn{6}{c	}{Arrows}	Scores
	1	2	3	4	5	6	
1							
2							
3							
4							
5							
6							
7							
8							
9							
10							
11							
12							
13							
14							

ARCHERY SCORE CARD

Name:

Date:

Distance (m):

Target Face (cm):

Team:

Round:

Ends	Arrows						Scores
	1	2	3	4	5	6	
1							
2							
3							
4							
5							
6							
7							
8							
9							
10							
11							
12							
13							
14							

ARCHERY SCORE CARD

Name:

Date:

Distance (m):   Team:

Target Face (cm):   Round:

Ends	Arrows						Scores
	1	2	3	4	5	6	
1							
2							
3							
4							
5							
6							
7							
8							
9							
10							
11							
12							
13							
14							

ARCHERY SCORE CARD

Name

Date

Distance (m)　　　　　　　Team

Target Face (cm)　　　　　Round

Ends	Arrows						Scores
	1	2	3	4	5	6	
1							
2							
3							
4							
5							
6							
7							
8							
9							
10							
11							
12							
13							
14							

ARCHERY SCORE CARD

Name:

Date:

Distance (m):   Team:

Target Face (cm):   Round:

Ends	\multicolumn{6}{c}{Arrows}	Scores
	1	2	3	4	5	6	
1							
2							
3							
4							
5							
6							
7							
8							
9							
10							
11							
12							
13							
14							

ARCHERY SCORE CARD

Name: _____

Date: _____

Distance (m): _____ Team: _____

Target Face (cm): _____ Round: _____

Ends	Arrows						Scores
	1	2	3	4	5	6	
1							
2							
3							
4							
5							
6							
7							
8							
9							
10							
11							
12							
13							
14							

ARCHERY SCORE CARD

Name:

Date:

Distance (m):   Team:

Target Face (cm):   Round:

Ends	Arrows						Scores
	1	2	3	4	5	6	
1							
2							
3							
4							
5							
6							
7							
8							
9							
10							
11							
12							
13							
14							

ARCHERY SCORE CARD

Name:

Date:

Distance (m):

Target Face (cm):

Team:

Round:

Ends	Arrows						Scores
	1	2	3	4	5	6	
1							
2							
3							
4							
5							
6							
7							
8							
9							
10							
11							
12							
13							
14							

ARCHERY SCORE CARD

Name	
Date	
Distance (m)	Team
Target Face (cm)	Round

Ends	Arrows						Scores
	1	2	3	4	5	6	
1							
2							
3							
4							
5							
6							
7							
8							
9							
10							
11							
12							
13							
14							

ARCHERY SCORE CARD

Name:

Date:

Distance (m): 　　　　　　Team:

Target Face (cm): 　　　　Round:

Ends	\multicolumn{6}{c	}{Arrows}	Scores
	1	2	3	4	5	6	
1							
2							
3							
4							
5							
6							
7							
8							
9							
10							
11							
12							
13							
14							

ARCHERY SCORE CARD

Name:

Date:

Distance (m):   Team:

Target Face (cm):   Round:

Ends	Arrows						Scores
	1	2	3	4	5	6	
1							
2							
3							
4							
5							
6							
7							
8							
9							
10							
11							
12							
13							
14							

ARCHERY SCORE CARD

Name:
Date:
Distance (m):
Target Face (cm):
Team:
Round:

Ends	\multicolumn{6}{c}{Arrows}	Scores
	1	2	3	4	5	6	
1							
2							
3							
4							
5							
6							
7							
8							
9							
10							
11							
12							
13							
14							

ARCHERY SCORE CARD

Name:
Date:
Distance (m):   Team:
Target Face (cm):   Round:

Ends	\multicolumn{6}{c	}{Arrows}	Scores
	1	2	3	4	5	6	
1							
2							
3							
4							
5							
6							
7							
8							
9							
10							
11							
12							
13							
14							

ARCHERY SCORE CARD

Name

Date

Distance (m)   Team

Target Face (cm)   Round

Ends	Arrows						Scores
	1	2	3	4	5	6	
1							
2							
3							
4							
5							
6							
7							
8							
9							
10							
11							
12							
13							
14							

ARCHERY SCORE CARD

Name:
Date:
Distance (m):
Target Face (cm):
Team:
Round:

Ends	Arrows						Scores
	1	2	3	4	5	6	
1							
2							
3							
4							
5							
6							
7							
8							
9							
10							
11							
12							
13							
14							

ARCHERY SCORE CARD

Name: _____

Date: _____

Distance (m): _____ Team: _____

Target Face (cm): _____ Round: _____

Ends	Arrows						Scores
	1	2	3	4	5	6	
1							
2							
3							
4							
5							
6							
7							
8							
9							
10							
11							
12							
13							
14							

ARCHERY SCORE CARD

Name:
Date:
Distance (m):
Target Face (cm):
Team:
Round:

Ends	Arrows						Scores
	1	2	3	4	5	6	
1							
2							
3							
4							
5							
6							
7							
8							
9							
10							
11							
12							
13							
14							

ARCHERY SCORE CARD

Name

Date

Distance (m)

Team

Target Face (cm)

Round

Ends	Arrows						Scores
	1	2	3	4	5	6	
1							
2							
3							
4							
5							
6							
7							
8							
9							
10							
11							
12							
13							
14							

ARCHERY SCORE CARD

Name:

Date:

Distance (m):

Target Face (cm):

Team:

Round:

Ends	Arrows						Scores
	1	2	3	4	5	6	
1							
2							
3							
4							
5							
6							
7							
8							
9							
10							
11							
12							
13							
14							

ARCHERY SCORE CARD

Name

Date

Distance (m)

Target Face (cm)

Team

Round

Ends	Arrows						Scores
	1	2	3	4	5	6	
1							
2							
3							
4							
5							
6							
7							
8							
9							
10							
11							
12							
13							
14							

ARCHERY SCORE CARD

Name:

Date:

Distance (m):

Target Face (cm):

Team:

Round:

Ends	Arrows						Scores
	1	2	3	4	5	6	
1							
2							
3							
4							
5							
6							
7							
8							
9							
10							
11							
12							
13							
14							

ARCHERY SCORE CARD

Name:

Date:

Distance (m):

Target Face (cm):

Team:

Round:

Ends	Arrows						Scores
	1	2	3	4	5	6	
1							
2							
3							
4							
5							
6							
7							
8							
9							
10							
11							
12							
13							
14							

ARCHERY SCORE CARD

Name:

Date:

Distance (m):   Team:

Target Face (cm):   Round:

Ends	Arrows						Scores
	1	2	3	4	5	6	
1							
2							
3							
4							
5							
6							
7							
8							
9							
10							
11							
12							
13							
14							

ARCHERY SCORE CARD

Name

Date

Distance (m)

Target Face (cm)

Team

Round

Ends	Arrows						Scores
	1	2	3	4	5	6	
1							
2							
3							
4							
5							
6							
7							
8							
9							
10							
11							
12							
13							
14							

ARCHERY SCORE CARD

Name:

Date:

Distance (m):   Team:

Target Face (cm):   Round:

Ends	Arrows						Scores
	1	2	3	4	5	6	
1							
2							
3							
4							
5							
6							
7							
8							
9							
10							
11							
12							
13							
14							

ARCHERY SCORE CARD

Name: _____

Date: _____

Distance (m): _____ Team: _____

Target Face (cm): _____ Round: _____

Ends	_____ Arrows _____						Scores
	1	2	3	4	5	6	
1							
2							
3							
4							
5							
6							
7							
8							
9							
10							
11							
12							
13							
14							

ARCHERY SCORE CARD

Name:

Date:

Distance (m):   Team:

Target Face (cm):   Round:

Ends	\multicolumn{6}{c	}{Arrows}	Scores
	1	2	3	4	5	6	
1							
2							
3							
4							
5							
6							
7							
8							
9							
10							
11							
12							
13							
14							

ARCHERY SCORE CARD

Name: _____

Date: _____

Distance (m): _____ Team: _____

Target Face (cm): _____ Round: _____

Ends	Arrows						Scores
	1	2	3	4	5	6	
1							
2							
3							
4							
5							
6							
7							
8							
9							
10							
11							
12							
13							
14							

ARCHERY SCORE CARD

Name:

Date:

Distance (m):   Team:

Target Face (cm):   Round:

Ends	Arrows						Scores
	1	2	3	4	5	6	
1							
2							
3							
4							
5							
6							
7							
8							
9							
10							
11							
12							
13							
14							

www.ingramcontent.com/pod-product-compliance
Lightning Source LLC
LaVergne TN
LVHW020445070526
838199LV00063B/4855